Where do we go from here?

John Blanchard

EVANGELICAL PRESS

EVANGELICAL PRESS,
Faverdale North, Darlington, DL3 0PH, England

e-mail: sales@evangelicalpress.org

Evangelical Press USA, P. O. Box 825, Webster, New York 14580, USA

e-mail: usa.sales@evangelicalpress.org

web: http://www.evangelicalpress.org

First published 2008

British Library Cataloguing in Publication Data available

ISBN-13 978-0-85234-679-2   ISBN 0 85234 679 4

Unless otherwise indicated, all Scripture quotations are from The Holy Bible, English
Standard Version, published by HarperCollins Publishers © 2001 by Crossway Bibles,
a division of Good News Publishers. Used by permission. All rights reserved.

Scripture quotations marked 'NIV' are from the Holy Bible, New International
Version. Copyright © 1973, 1978, 1984, International Bible Society. Used by permission of Hodder & Stoughton, a member of the Hodder Headline Group. All rights
reserved. 'NIV' is a registered trademark of International Bible Society, UK trademark
number 1448790.

Printed and bound in Great Britain by Pennyprint, Dunston, Tyne & Wear

Where do we go from here?

The haemorrhage had gradually spread to the rest of the brain. Since his heart was healthy and strong, it affected the breathing centres bit by bit and caused suffocation. For the last twelve hours the lack of oxygen was acute. His face altered and became dark. His lips turned black and the features grew unrecognizable. The last hours were nothing but slow strangulation. The death agony was horrible. He literally choked to death as we watched.

At what seemed like the very last moment he suddenly opened his eyes and cast a glance over everyone in the room. It was a terrible glance, insane or perhaps angry, and full of fear of death and the unfamiliar faces of the doctors bent over him. The glance swept over everyone in a second.

Then something incomprehensible and awesome happened, that to this day I can't forget and don't understand. He suddenly lifted his left hand as though bringing down a curse on us all. The gesture was incomprehensible and full of menace, and no one could say to whom or what it might be directed. The next moment, after a final effort, the spirit wrenched itself free of the flesh.[1]

These moving words come from the book *Twenty Letters to a Friend*, the autobiography of Svetlana Alliluyeva, youngest child and only daughter of the man whose last earthly moments she was so vividly describing. Born Iosif Vissarionovich Dzhugashvili, he called himself Joseph Stalin ('Man of Steel') and was the undisputed dictator of some 285,000,000 people living in the Soviet Union. For some twenty-four years his word was law and had the power of life and death, wiping out millions of people who opposed his political or religious convictions. Tens of thousands of priests, monks and nuns were persecuted and killed, with over 100,000 shot during the purges of 1937–1938. At the peak of his career he was arguably the most powerful man on earth, yet was eventually reduced to a feeble physical wreck, and on 5 March 1953 he was forced to yield to a more powerful enemy that would not be denied — death.

What makes our opening paragraph so arresting is not the writer or the subject, but the event it describes, the moment of a person's death — an event made irresistibly compelling because every human being on our planet is moving towards his or her own appointment with it at the rate of twenty-four hours a day. There is a growing interest in subjects associated with death, such as spiritism, life beyond the grave, psychic communication with the dead, astral projection and various occult practices, though millions of people who are drawn to these things fail to get to grips with the matter of death itself.

Yet death is inescapable, and what we call living could equally well be called dying. We could rightly say that the whole world is a hospital and every person in it a terminal patient. Death is no respecter of persons. It comes to young and old, rich and poor, good and bad, educated and ignorant. It knows no colour bar and runs no means test. From kings to commoners, all must eventually bow to it. 'Superstars' and 'nonentities' share the same fate. Alexander the Great once found his philosopher friend Diogenes standing in a field, looking intently at a large pile of bones. Asked what he was doing, the old man turned to Alexander and replied, 'I am searching for the bones of your father Philip, but I cannot seem to distinguish them from the bones of the slaves.' From the greatest to the least, from the most beautiful to the most plain, from the richest to the poorest, death is the universal equalizer.

Nor is death a respecter of time or place. It strikes at every minute of day and night, claiming its victims on land, on sea, in the air, in the hospital bed, the office, the supermarket and the armchair, on the open road, the sports field and in the study. Even cutting-edge science is unable to deny it; 'wonder drugs', intensive care and spare-part surgery must all eventually give way to its demands. For both the writer and reader of these words our last appointment in life is one we will not make yet cannot avoid. We can take regular exercise, eat nothing but 'health foods', swallow vitamin pills and other food supplements on a daily basis, have regular medical check-ups and follow the best possible advice in micro-managing our lifestyle, yet the best we can do is to postpone the inevitable — and you are twenty-four hours nearer that appointment than at this time yesterday.

For countless other people the inescapable fact of death is so unpalatable that a truckload of terms have been invented to avoid using the dreaded 'D...' word. Australian Museum Online has a website called 'Death — The Last Taboo'. In the 1970s the English anthropologist Geoffrey Gorer claimed, 'The truth of the matter is that death has replaced sex as the forbidden subject of conversation in polite society,' and this is certainly true today. Sex is gratuitously dragged into more films, television and radio programmes, books, magazines, advertising and conversations than ever before, while death is carefully sidelined. We say that someone has 'passed away', 'moved on', or 'is no longer with us'. Numerous internet websites reflect a stream of euphemisms, with death described as 'the big sleep', 'crossing the river' and 'the end of the line', while being dead is called being 'six feet under', 'de-animated' or even having 'left the room'. Some people trivialize the issue by referring to those who have 'kicked the bucket', 'popped their clogs', 'snuffed it', 'croaked', 'pegged out', 'bitten the dust', 'cashed in their chips', or 'fallen off the twig'. In the United States undertakers are frequently referred to as 'grief therapists', funeral homes as 'slumber rooms', cemeteries as 'memorial parks' and gravestones as 'horizontal markers'. Some hospitals even go so far as to refer to the death of a patient as 'negative patient care outcome', which states the truth while hiding the word that nobody wants to hear.

The fear factor

Avoiding the subject shows that almost as universal as the fact of death is *the fear of death*. The American film producer Woody Allen famously said, 'I'm not afraid of dying. I just don't want to be there when it happens,' but this was just his quirky way of twisting the truth. The eighteenth-century French thinker Jean-Jacques Rousseau was nearer the mark when he claimed, 'He who pretends to face death without fear is a liar,' and the Bible is not exaggerating when it speaks of men being 'brought to the king of terrors' (Job 18:14).This explains people's reluctance to talk about death, and their concern to drive it from their minds. Death troubles and torments them, frustrates and frightens them, the Bible going so far as to say that 'through fear of death' some people are 'subject to slavery' (Hebrews 2:15).

One of the most obvious reasons for the dread of death is *the fear of pain.* The English priest and poet G. Studdert Kennedy once said that a person who is not disturbed by the problem of pain is suffering from hardening of the heart or softening of the brain. A whole encyclopaedia of ailments such as toothache, migraine, arthritis, sciatica and pleurisy can cause pain, which at times can be severe, though most causes of pain are not terminal and many respond to treatment. However, nobody in their right senses can look forward to the prospect of months, or even years, of pain, knowing that things will steadily get worse and bring life to an agonizing end.

Then there is *the fear of personal loss.* At the end of one of his most profitable years on the European Tour, the English professional golfer Simon Dyson was asked, 'Is there anything that frightens you?' Dyson replied, 'Death. I'm in a position now where I can pretty much do as I want… Dying wouldn't be good right now.'[2] The prospect of losing all of their possessions is something many people dread.

Another is *fear of the unknown.* Whatever our social status, we all live in a world with which we are familiar, every day filled with sights and sounds that give us a sense of belonging. We are surrounded by our chosen possessions; we have a comfortable circle of friends, and our minds are crowded with our personal hopes, ambitions, plans and dreams. Death removes all of these and propels us into unknown territory, where everything is a dark and fearful void, with no signposts or landmarks. It is little wonder that for countless people this is a frightening prospect.

Then there is *the fear of meeting God.* For millions of people who give little thought to him (except, perhaps, when attending a funeral) there is from time to time the nagging and disturbing instinct that they will one day have to meet their Maker. The British racing driver Stirling Moss won sixteen Formula One Grands Prix and has been called 'the greatest driver never to win the World Championship'. He was known for his great courage and daring on the racetrack, yet when he was at the height of his fame he told a newspaper reporter, 'I am frightened of death. I know it means going to meet one's Maker, and one shouldn't be afraid of that. But I am.'

Tied in to this is *the fear of final judgement*. On a BBC radio programme the well-known humanist Marghanita Laski was asked what were the most important issues that any person had to face. She replied, 'We are lonely, we are guilty and we are going to die.' Linking guilt and death together points to the influence of the conscience and to the fact that more people than would readily admit it have a gnawing fear that coming face to face with God will not be party time. Instead, it will be a moment when their lives will come under the searching review of one who is utterly holy and who has said of the kingdom of heaven that 'Nothing unclean will ever enter it' (Revelation 21:27). In the words of the contemporary British theologian J. I. Packer, 'No man is entirely without inklings of judgement.'[3]

The Bible gives several vivid examples of man's fear of God's judgement, both in this life and the life to come. When Israel's King Saul was told by the prophet Samuel that because of his sin God would deliver him and his nation into the hands of their bitter enemies the Philistines, he 'fell at once full length on the ground, filled with fear' (1 Samuel 28:20). When the apostle Paul spoke to Felix, the heathen governor of Judea, about 'righteousness and self-control and the coming judgement', the ruler was 'alarmed' (Acts 24:25). In one of the most dramatic passages in the Bible we are given a glimpse of the moment when godless multitudes meet their Maker: 'Then the kings of earth and the great ones and the generals and the rich and the powerful ones, and everyone, slave and free, hid themselves in the caves and among the rocks of the mountains, calling to the mountains and rocks, "Fall on us and hide us from the face of him who is seated on the throne, and from the wrath of the Lamb, for the great day of their wrath has come, and who can stand?"' (Revelation 6:15-17).

Should this surprise us? Surely there could be nothing more terrifying than to know that when death strikes (as it could at any time and without a moment's notice) it would bring us face to face with a righteous and holy

God *in our present moral and spiritual condition* and with no further opportunity to put things right?

Death is the ultimate reality for every human being, and the only sane approach is to face it honestly, examine it carefully and prepare for it wisely. This booklet has been written to help you do all three of these things, guided not by human speculation but by the clear light of the Bible, 'the living and abiding word of God' (1 Peter 1:23).

Tackling the truth

The Bible begins to tackle the subject by stating two undeniable truths. The first is *the certainty of death.* In the Old Testament the point is made by three of the finest men on its pages. Job called death 'the house appointed for all living' (Job 30:23); King David asked the rhetorical question, 'What man can live and never see death?' (Psalm 89:48), while King Solomon bluntly stated, 'No man has power to retain the spirit, or power over the day of death' (Ecclesiastes 8:8).

In a memorable phrase earlier in his book, Solomon also said, 'For everything there is a season, and a time for every matter under heaven' (Ecclesiastes 3:1). He then listed fourteen couplets, the first of which says that there is 'a time to be born and a time to die' (Ecclesiastes 3:2). There is more to this phrase than meets the eye, as the word 'time' refers not merely to the certainty of death, but to exactly when the event will take place. The writer is saying that the exact date of his death was set in God's calendar as surely as the date of his birth. For everyone now living on earth there is 'a time to die' — *God's time.*

Secondly, the Bible uses vivid metaphors to warn us of *the brevity of life.* It says, 'You are a mist that appears for a little time and then vanishes' (James 4:14), that our days on earth are 'swifter than a weaver's shuttle' (Job 7:6) and 'swifter than a runner' (Job 9:25), and that they are 'like a shadow' (1 Chronicles 29:15). In our early years these images might seem like 'scare stories' and in middle age our lives are cluttered with so many things that we scarcely give them much attention. Yet they are strikingly true and we should bear them in mind at every stage of life, remembering that, as the twelfth-century theologian Bernard of Clairvaux vividly put it, 'Death is oftentimes as near to the young man's back as it is to the old man's face.'[4]

Travelling as extensively as I do in the course of my ministry, I am often asked, 'Where do you go from here?' The question we are facing in this booklet is much more serious. It is not asking where we are planning to go tomorrow, next week or next year, but where we go when our last day on earth is over. People have come up with all kinds of answers to that question, but anyone who ignores it altogether is simply not thinking straight.

Who knows?

One approach to the subject is to settle for *agnosticism*, which says that what happens after death is a complete mystery. This was the line taken by the sixteenth-century Frenchman François Rabelais. At one time or another he was a monk, a student of law and astronomy, a doctor and a writer famous for his bawdy humour, yet as he reached the end of a life packed with incident his last words were: 'I am off in search of a great Perhaps.' A century later the English philosopher Thomas Hobbes spoke of his coming death as taking 'my last voyage, a great leap in the dark'.[5]

Others have expressed the same kind of thing in a more light-hearted way. In the last chapter of his book *Around the World in 81 Years*, the British comedy actor Robert Morley wrote, 'If, as I have always thought, life is a party, I should be leaving quite soon… I'll just collect my shroud and be off. Where to exactly? Is there another party just up the road?'[6] He 'collected his shroud' on 3 June 1992, but he need not have been uncertain as to what would happen afterwards. It is certainly true that, left to ourselves, there is nothing we can possibly know about what lies beyond the grave — but we are not left to ourselves. God has not left us in the dark; in the Bible he has revealed all that we need to know about what happens after we have drawn our final breath.

The end?

A second idea has been around for thousands of years and says that death results in *annihilation*. The Greek philosopher Aristotle, who died in 322 BC, wrote that death is 'to be the most feared of all things … for it appears to be the end of everything'.[7] About fifty years later Epicurus, another Greek philosopher, dismissed death as being 'of no concern to us; for while we exist death is not present, and when death is present we no longer exist'.[8] The twentieth-century British thinker Bertrand Russell expressed the same idea when he said that 'All the noonday brightness of human genius is doomed to extinction.'[9] Countless others wonder whether this might be the case. In his 2007 volume *More Time for Politics*, the British politician Tony Benn writes of grieving over the death of his wife Caroline a year after the event: 'I wondered where Caroline was. Had she disappeared into thin air? What does death mean? Is it a complete and absolute end?'[10]

Secular humanism, which sees man at the centre of everything, has no doubts about the answer to that last question, and a spokesman for the British Humanist Association writes, 'Life leads to nothing, and every pretence that it does not is a deceit.'[11] Likening death to people crossing a bridge, he went on to say, 'The bridge leads nowhere, and those who are pressing forward to cross it are going nowhere.'[12] The Beatles' singer John Lennon reflected the same idea in his hit song *Imagine*:

Imagine there's no heaven;
It's easy if you try.
No hell below us,
Above us only sky.
Imagine all the people
Living for today. [13]

It is not difficult to see some kind of attraction in this idea, not least because it relieves moral pressure. If we are extinguished when we die, we might as well grasp every ounce of pleasure while we can; as followers of Epicurus put it, let us 'eat, drink and be merry, for tomorrow we die'. What is more, we need not be too squeamish about how we get what we want, regardless of how it affects other people. Yet if we take the idea of annihilation to its logical conclusion it means that there will never be any final righting of wrongs, no eternal justice. The serial killer and the child who dies in infancy, the ruthless dictator and the gentle, law-abiding citizen, the rapist and his violated victim will all have the same destiny in being wiped out of existence the moment they die.

Annihilation is enthusiastically endorsed by atheists, but it cancels out humankind's universal and self-conscious sense of special worth and dignity, the conviction that we are of greater value than any other living being on our planet. Atheism says that we begin as a fluke, live as a farce and end as fertilizer, yet if forced to choose between saving the life of a human being or a dog, I know of nobody who would choose the dog. The twentieth-century American theologian Francis Schaeffer said it well: 'All men ... have a deep longing for significance, a longing for meaning ... no man, regardless of his theoretical system, is content to look at himself as a finally meaningless machine which can and will be discarded totally and for ever.'[14] There is something radically wrong with a person who has no sense of personal worth or dignity and who thinks that a few years spent on this planet is the sum total of what he or she can expect. The British preacher David Watson told of speaking to a medical student who had just dissected his first human corpse, the body lying there like a lifeless wax model as he cut away various organs. Still shaken by the experience, he told Watson, 'If this is all that we become at death, what is the point of anything?'[15]

Yet the clinching argument against the idea that death is the end comes from the Bible, in which the creation story reaches a climax with the words:

So God created man in his own image,
  in the image of God he created him;
  male and female he created them

(Genesis 1:27).

Nothing else living on our planet is said to have been created 'in the image of God' and, as 'God is spirit' (John 4:24) and has no size or shape, to be created in his image obviously means something beyond the physical. It means that man is both personal and spiritual, created for fellowship with his Maker 'in a way totally surpassing that of any other earthly being'.[16] Without being divine, man was created with qualities that enabled him to do in a finite way what God does in an infinite way. As the contemporary British preacher Peter Lewis says, 'Human uniqueness consists not in the fact that we talk with each other, rather that God talks to us and invites us to reply.'[17] As human beings we are not meaningless accidents of mindless evolution, or 'jumped-up apes', but moral and spiritual beings with meaning, purpose and destiny.

The Bible summarizes this truth by saying that God 'has put eternity into man's heart' (Ecclesiastes 3:11), something illustrated by the American author Sheldon Vanauken in his delightful book *A Severe Mercy*. Vanauken says that while 'time' is such a precious commodity to man, we always seem to be fighting against it, whereas animals seem totally untroubled by time and act as if it was their natural environment. He goes on to say that as humans we have 'a kind of appetite for eternity', suggesting that we have not always been, or will not always be, temporal creatures: 'It suggests that *we were created for eternity*... Where, we cry, has the time gone? We aren't adapted to it, not at home in it. If that is so, it may appear as proof, or at least a powerful suggestion, that *eternity exists and is our home*.'[18] This fits perfectly with the Bible's clear statement that at a person's death, 'The dust returns to the earth as it was, and the spirit returns to God who gave it' (Ecclesiastes 12:7).

I have taken some time looking at the idea that we are annihilated at death, because countless people are taken in by it. Yet the Bible says nothing to back it up and a great deal to refute it. In a phrase, the Bible annihilates annihilation.

Everybody home?

A third idea — *universalism* —is equally popular — and for an even more obvious reason. It claims to have a very different basis, because instead of rejecting the Bible it relies on it, at least to the extent of accepting what it says about our creation by God, our moral responsibility throughout life and the certainty of our final judgement. It then leans heavily on the fact that 'God is love' (1 John 4:8) and says that regardless of the kind of life we have lived, God will wrap his arms around us and receive us into heaven, turning a blind eye to all our failings. Everyone will be welcomed in the same way, even those who showed no religious inclinations while on earth. In July 1978, the BBC's senior golf commentator Henry Longhurst lay dying of terminal cancer at his home in England. When his colleague Peter Alliss telephoned him from Hawaii, Longhurst told him, 'I'm very near the end now. I've never been a very religious man, but I know you and I will meet again, many years from now, in another place. The one good thing about me going first is that at least it will afford me the opportunity of finding the sponsor's hospitality room.'[19] This is universalism at its simplest, and millions of people share Longhurst's dream, even if they are not able to express it with such a light touch. The natural fear of dying is overcome by the belief that on the other side of the grave God will welcome us with open arms and without the need for us to pass any entrance examination, regardless of what we have believed and how we have behaved. In order to get to heaven all we have to do is die. One liberal theologian said that dying is rather like approaching a customs post, nervously hoping that officials will not spot the contraband we are carrying, only to find that when we get there the post is deserted and we can march straight through.

It is easy to see why countless millions sign up to universalism. As the American theologian R. C. Sproul puts it, 'God is viewed as being so "loving" that he really doesn't care too much if we keep his law. The law is there to guide us, but if we stumble and fall, our celestial grandfather will merely wink and say, "Boys will be boys." '[20]

According to universalism, even those whose actions outraged society will be treated in the same way, with death acting as a kind of divine detergent, giving everybody a clean bill of moral and spiritual health. Identical twin brothers Ronnie and Reggie Kray were London's most notorious gang leaders for about twenty years, heavily involved in armed robberies, arson, protection rackets, violent assault and murder. Yet their contacts with politicians and media personalities gave them an aura of stardom and when

Ronnie Kray died on 17 March 1995 one newspaper reporter wrote, 'His sins, which were many, were forgiven and forgotten the moment he met God.'

Universalism is understandably popular, but there is not a single trace of the idea in the Bible. Instead, it divides people between those who are 'saved' (Romans 10:13) and those who are 'lost' (Luke 19:10); between those who are in 'the light' (Isaiah 2:5) and those who are in 'darkness' (Proverbs 4:19); between those who beyond the grave will experience 'eternal life' and those who will experience 'eternal punishment' (Matthew 25:46). To believe that after death there will be prizes for everybody and punishment for nobody is to fly in the face of what the Bible teaches. Far from guaranteeing eternal life for everybody, God says, 'Behold I set before you the way of life and the way of death' (Jeremiah 21:8). What is more, he also gives us a clear instruction and an equally clear warning: 'Enter by the narrow gate. For the gate is wide and the way is easy that leads to destruction, and those who enter by it are many. For the gate is narrow and the way is hard that leads to life, and those who find it are few' (Matthew 7:13-14). In the light of these statements, the idea that we will all 'live happily ever after' has no more credibility than a fairy tale. We dare not rely on it.

Recycling?

Reincarnation (which literally means 'to be made flesh again') is another suggestion as to what happens after death. Reincarnation says that when a person dies he or she is 'recycled' and returns to earth as a different kind of person, or even as an animal, a bird, a reptile or an insect, their new status depending on their previous quality of life. Reincarnation has a long history and, with a number of complex variations, forms an important part of Hinduism, Buddhism, Sikhism and Taoism. The New Age Movement teaches repeated reincarnations as a spiritual path or *sadhana*, which is rarely completed during a single earthly lifetime. Reincarnation in one form or another is also to be found in Theosophy, Spiritism, Scientism, New Thought, Rosicrucianism, Anthroposophy and a number of other religions and cults. Even people with no attachment to any of these have more than a sneaking suspicion that there might be something in the idea. A golfing partner once told me about a delightful neighbour of his who had died, then added, 'Some time later a beautiful bird began appearing regularly in my garden and I am certain that this is my neighbour come back to earth.'

Recent polls indicate that 20% of Americans and 33% of Europeans believe in reincarnation. One organization promoting reincarnation has a website which claims that if people log on and answer a series of questions 'honestly' it will forecast what form they will take when they return to earth. Most reincarnation models relate to *karma* ('act', 'action' or 'performance') and the law of cause and effect. A person accumulating good *karma* will be reincarnated in a higher state, whereas a person accumulating bad *karma* will be reincarnated in a lower state. As the American actress Shirley MacLaine, a passionate New Ager, put it, 'Reincarnation is like show business. You just keep doing it until you get it right.' The concept of reincarnation seems to offer an attractive explanation of humanity's origin and destiny. To know that you lived many previous lives and that there are others to come may seem to offer some kind of perspective from which to judge the meaning of life. It also seems to offer endless chances to 'get it right'. Many are attracted to it because it seems to explain why some people seem in permanent good health while others fight constant battles with illness, and why some easily become wealthy while others struggle against poverty.

When we turn to the Bible we find the idea of reincarnation refuted point-blank. The Old Testament states, 'He who goes down to the grave does not return' (Job 7:9, NIV), while the New Testament simply confirms that 'It is appointed for man to die *once*' (Hebrews 9:27, emphasis added). There is not the remotest possibility of smuggling reincarnation into either of these statements. Our life on earth is a one-way street — and death is not a revolving door.

Defining death

Having looked at some of the wrong answers to the question posed in our title, we are now in a position to tackle it in the clear light of what the Bible says, and the best place to begin is with the nature and meaning of death itself. Until fairly recently determining the precise moment of a person's death was thought to be simple and straightforward: it was when the heart stopped beating and the lungs stopped functioning. However, we now live in an age of heart transplantation, and in a bizarre case in California a man accused of murder defended himself on the grounds that his victim was not dead because his heart was beating in someone else's body![21]

Today, doctors and clinicians usually talk about 'brain death' or 'biological death'. A person is considered dead when electrical activity in the whole brain comes to an end, though this may well be medically redefined in the future. Be that as it may, the Bible gives a definition that we all know to be accurate. In the Old Testament, Jacob's wife Rachel is said to have been dying when 'her soul was departing' (Genesis 35:18), while in the New Testament the death of Jesus is the moment when he 'gave up his spirit' (John 19:30). Elsewhere, the same point is made in the straightforward statement that 'The body apart from the spirit is dead' (James 2:26). Without the spirit a human body becomes a corpse.

Where is the body?

This division between body and spirit means that we can begin to answer the question, 'Where do we go from here?', by concentrating first on what happens to the human *body* after death, and the answer is fairly simple. In most cultures it undergoes some kind of ritual disposal, normally burial or cremation. Burial is usually a straightforward procedure, but in the case of a person of special note, it could be in some kind of crypt, sepulchre or mausoleum, of which the Taj Mahal in India and the Egyptian pyramids are examples. In some cultures, the corpse is left on high ground for animals or birds of prey to dispose of. Burial at sea is another option, as is space burial, in which the cremated remains of the body are launched into orbit.

Whichever method of disposal is chosen, it confirms what God told the first human being on the planet: 'You are dust, and to dust you shall return' (Genesis 3:19).This looks back to man's original creation, the Bible telling us that 'The LORD God formed the man of dust from the ground and breathed into his nostrils the breath of life, and the man became a living creature' (Genesis 2:7). Incidentally, this tells us that man is not the result of millions of years of evolution, but comes directly from the earth, with no succession of lower creatures intervening, while at death his body returns to its original state. In modern terms, our bodies are biodegradable; in the Puritans' direct language, we become 'worms' meat'. Peter Lewis has it exactly right when he says, 'Death itself will bring to dust the person who was made from dust but who was not made to die.'[22]

Whatever the type of funeral, we treat a loved one's body with great respect, doing all we can to ensure that it is disposed of with reverence and care. Even after burial or cremation our natural instinct is to believe that the remains are important, though this sometimes produces bizarre results. In May 1990 an English national newspaper carried the story of Arthur Strange, who as a young man had played football for his local club, Dorchester Town F. C., and remained a loyal supporter long after his playing days were over. After his death and cremation his family respected his wish that his ashes be scattered in the centre circle of the club's ground. Some years later supermarket owners bought the property and the football club moved to a new venue. This brought a huge profit for the club, but as the redevelopment of the site got under way the families of Arthur Strange and of several other fans whose ashes had been scattered on the pitch agonized over the precise location of their remains. Eventually, some soil was taken from the old football pitch and arranged in a symbolic cross in the centre circle of the new one. After officiating at the ceremony the club's chaplain told the press, 'What people did not want was their relatives under the fish counter at Tesco's.'[23]

This flags up something that is vitally important for us to grasp — namely the Bible's teaching that *'death' never means the end.* Whenever the Bible speaks of death, it means separation, *not termination.* Francis Schaeffer easily illustrates this in relation to a person approaching the very end of life: 'Watch a man as he dies. *Five minutes later he still exists.* There is no such thing as stopping the existence of a man. He still goes on. He has not lost his being as a human being. He has not lost things which he intrinsically is as a man. He has not become an animal or a machine.'[24] This came home to me in an intensely personal way on 2 July 1990 in the Princess Elizabeth Hospital, Guernsey. My elderly stepmother had undergone a very serious operation and was obviously nearing the end of her life. As I held her hand and prayed for her we were able to share a few words (her last ones being, 'I love you and I love Jesus') and then she quietly breathed her last. Yet that did not mean that she no longer existed. A human being is not a body without a soul, nor a soul without a body, but is both body and soul. In my stepmother's case, the two had been separated, but her now lifeless body was proof that she had not been annihilated. Nothing could more clearly demonstrate that death is not termination, but separation — in the case of physical death the separation of the soul from the body.

Where is the soul?

Having answered the more straightforward question, 'Where does the body go from here?', we obviously need to answer another one: 'Where does the soul go from here?' There are many ideas about this, one of the most popular being that after death the soul 'sleeps', at least until some future date, a view held among some minority sects and cults claiming to be part of the Christian church. It seems to offer some kind of comfort to those who have been bereaved, but we dare not settle for an answer that is driven only, or mainly, by our own emotional needs. Once again, we must rely only on the Bible to give us the right answer to the question.

When we turn to the Bible we find it telling us that the souls of those who have died remain alive and conscious in what theologians refer to as an 'intermediate state'. The Bible certainly speaks of the dead as those who 'sank into sleep' (Psalm 76:5) and related language is used about forty times in the Old Testament. There are similar references in the New Testament, including the record of Stephen, the first Christian martyr. Stoned to death by opponents of his gospel preaching, he uttered a final prayer, 'Lord, do not hold this sin against them,' and then he 'fell asleep' (Acts 7:60).

At first glance, these statements do seem to mean 'soul sleep', but there are powerful arguments against it. The first is the Bible's teaching that what 'falls asleep' when someone dies is the *person*, in the sense that he or she takes no further part in any conscious earthly activities. As this absence of conscious activity is what happens when someone falls asleep at night (or at any other time) the language is a perfect fit for what happens at death. It is hugely important to understand that in using 'sleep' as a synonym for death, the Bible is using pictorial language, not making a theological statement. A dead person gives every appearance of being asleep, and there are times when for a few seconds it is difficult to make the distinction. Just after my stepmother died, nurses came into the ward to change her position and make her more comfortable, and it took a few moments for them to realize that she had died.

Secondly, the Bible consistently teaches that the soul is *conscious* after death. This is established in a story Jesus told about two men whose lives had been very different (see Luke 16:19-31). The first was a rich but godless man who died and was buried and was 'in torment' in 'Hades' (verse 23). The second was a poor but apparently godly man who 'died and was carried by the angels to Abraham's side' (verse 22). 'Hades' clearly means a place of punishment for the ungodly, while, as Abraham was universally recognized as 'the father of all who believe' (Romans 4:11), 'Abraham's side' — a phrase not used anywhere else in the Bible — obviously means a place of great bliss.

There is no need to examine the details and meaning of the story here, except to note that a great deal of it involves the rich man seeing and speaking. As his body had been buried and therefore lay somewhere underground here on earth, the language is clearly metaphorical and relates to his soul, which must have been conscious, as it was able to feel the pain of the torment in which he found himself. It is impossible to deny that both the rich man (in Hades) and the poor man (at Abraham's side) were alive, even though at that stage their bodies were in earthly graves.

Another passage makes the same point about the consciousness of the deceased in a more positive way. In a discussion with Sadducees, members of a priestly sect who did not believe in life after death, Jesus quoted an Old Testament passage in which God told Moses, 'I am the God of Abraham, and the God of Isaac, and the God of Jacob,' before adding, 'He [God] is not God of the dead, but of the living' (Mark 12:26-27). Yet as he spoke the bodies of these three patriarchs were decomposing in graves at Hebron, about thirty kilometres to the south.

We need to summarize this important section before we move on. Whatever other divisions we may make for social or other reasons, the Bible divides humankind into two groups. It uses a number of names for these, including 'the righteous' (Romans 1:17) and 'the 'unrighteous' (2 Peter 2:9). If we were to read the entire Bible we would find that 'the righteous' are those who have come into a living relationship with God and seek to serve and obey him, while the description 'the unrighteous' refers to those (many of whom may be religious and outwardly respectable) who have never come into such a relationship. After death, the souls of the righteous are 'at Abraham's side' — on one occasion Jesus called it 'Paradise' (Luke 23:43) — a place of unimaginable delight. The souls of the unrighteous are in Hades, where they are kept 'under punishment until the day of judgement' (2 Peter 2:9). In the fullest biblical meaning of the words, therefore, the righteous are not in heaven at this point and the unrighteous are not in hell. As illustrations we could say that the righteous are in the palace, waiting to enter the throne room, while the unrighteous are remanded in custody, waiting to receive their final sentence. But before either reaches their ultimate destiny, a truly momentous event will take place — one that will also affect those who are still living on earth when it happens.

The return

Of all the Bible's doctrines, there is one that is often misunderstood by Christians and often ridiculed by unbelievers: the return of the Lord Jesus Christ to the earth, commonly called the Second Coming.

It is not too difficult to see why it has such a bad press among unbelievers. In the first place, the idea that a human being who was dead and buried about 2,000 years ago will suddenly reappear, apparently from outer space, seems like science fiction rather than anything to be taken seriously. Secondly, many heretical cults major on 'end of the world' scenarios, some including the Second Coming of Christ, but most people have inbuilt suspicions about 'fringe religions'. Then there has been so much erroneous speculation about the timing of the end of the world. There was great excitement as the year 1000 approached (presumably among those who imagined that God would deal in nice round numbers!). For other reasons 1260 was wrongly earmarked. A Roman Catholic priest wrote a book prophesying that the world would end in 1847; he was given permission to publish it in 1848! Jehovah's Witnesses got it wrong at least four times, in 1874, 1914, 1915 and 1975. In 1988 Edgar Whisenant, from Little Rock, Arkansas, published a book listing eighty-eight reasons why Jesus would return in 1988 — on 11, 12 or 13 September. As the year 2000 approached, several groups began to focus on 'the end times'. These included the notorious Branch Davidians, eighty-two of whose members were eventually killed near Waco, Texas, during a siege by United States government agents.

The Bible paints a very different picture. As far as the future history of the world is concerned, nothing is stated more often or more emphatically than the Second Coming of Christ. It is mentioned no fewer than 300 times in the New Testament alone, which works out at once in every thirteen verses from Matthew to Revelation. When the Japanese armies forced American and Filipino troops to withdraw from the Philippines in May 1942, the American General Douglas MacArthur promised the islanders, 'I shall return,' and had the message printed on chocolate bars, cigarette packets, matchboxes and thousands of other items, then had them scattered all over the islands to underline his promise, which he kept less than three years later. The greater promise of the Second Coming of Christ is scattered all over the New Testament, with every writer making reference to it, never once as a speculation but always as a certainty.

The apostle Paul says, 'The Lord himself will descend from heaven with a cry of command, with the voice of an archangel, and with the sound of the trumpet of God' (1 Thessalonians 4:16). James writes about 'the coming of the Lord' (James 5:7). Peter emphasizes its certainty by telling his readers, 'For we did not follow cleverly devised myths when we made known to you the power and coming of our Lord Jesus Christ ' (2 Peter 1:16). Using one of his own favourite titles for himself — 'the Son of Man' — Jesus assured his followers, 'The Son of Man is going to come with his angels in the glory of his Father' (Matthew 16:27). On another occasion he counselled one of his enemies, 'You will see the Son of Man seated at the right hand of Power, and coming with the clouds of heaven' (Mark 14:62). Elsewhere, he warned his critics that 'Whoever is ashamed of me and of my words, of him will the Son of Man be ashamed when he comes in his glory and the glory of the Father and of the holy angels' (Luke 9:26).

Even among those who believe the Bible, there has been widespread confusion about the exact meaning of certain events that will occur at that time, and countless books have been written to 'prove' one point or another, but these have no bearing on our present question. There are just three points on which we need to be clear before we go any further.

The first is that *he will return suddenly and unexpectedly*, as Jesus made clear in a series of vivid illustrations. He said that his return would be 'as the lightning comes from the east and shines as far as the west' (Matthew 24:27) and like a thief breaking into a house at night (see Matthew 24:42-44). It will begin like every other day, with people 'eating and drinking, marrying and giving in marriage' (Matthew 24:38). It will be a day when there will be countless births, marriages and deaths. Some people will fall in love and others will get divorced; some will get promotion and others will be made redundant; some will be admitted to hospital and others will be discharged; for some it will be just 'another day in the office' and for others a day of great excitement. In other words, it will be 'business as usual'.

The second is that *all speculation as to when this will happen is groundless and foolish,* because, as Jesus himself said, 'Concerning that day or that hour, no one knows' (Mark 13:32). We need therefore take no notice of anyone who claims to know exactly when Jesus will return to the earth.

The third is that *when it does happen, 'every eye will see him'* (Revelation 1:7). Many people living at the time will be shocked and amazed at his return, but nobody will be in any doubt about it. The return of Jesus to the earth will not be like his first coming as a baby, which took place in a small town in the Middle East and led to the beginnings of a movement that gradually spread its way around the world over the centuries. Instead, it will be universal and instantaneous, something that will 'transcend all events in space and time hitherto experienced'.[25] It will be dynamic, dramatic and decisive, as it propels all of humanity towards its final destiny.

It would be difficult to improve on what C. S. Lewis has to say on the Second Coming of Christ:

I wonder whether people who ask God to interfere openly and directly in our world quite realize what it will be like when he does. God's going to invade all right. When that happens, it's the end of the world. When the Author walks onto the stage, the play's over. For this time it will be so overwhelming that it will strike either irresistible love or irresistible horror into every creature. It will be too late then to choose your sides... It will be the time when we discover which side we have really chosen, whether we realize it or not.[26]

Whole again

By now you may be asking, 'But what has all of this to do with my own future? What will happen to me when he comes?' Whether you are alive or dead at that moment, the answer depends on your standing with God when the Second Coming happens! On the day Jesus returns to the earth billions of people will obviously have already died, while billions of others will still be alive and going about their daily routines. The Second Coming will radically change things for both the living and the dead.

As far as the dead are concerned, their bodies will be raised again to life. In the Bible's words, when Jesus returns, 'All who are in the tombs will hear his voice and come out' (John 5:28-29). However they may be disposed of and however much they disintegrate, no bodies are ever annihilated, and at the Second Coming they will all be brought back to life.

Some people will ask, 'But how is this possible? What about the countless millions of people who are cremated and whose bodies are reduced to a handful of ashes? What about people whose buried bodies have been decomposing for thousands of years? What about those lost or buried at sea, swept away in a hurricane, buried in avalanches, blown to pieces in mid-air, or vaporized in the atomic blasts at Hiroshima and Nagasaki? What about those who lost limbs years before dying or who had organ transplants? How can all of this fit into the idea that people's entire bodies will not only be made whole but reintegrated with their souls so that they are once again complete human beings?' The contemporary British preacher John Benton easily shows that these questions betray ignorance of God's power and purpose. After explaining that a teacher can write on a blackboard, rub off what he or she has written, and then *write the same words or figures again*, Benton adds, 'God is able to rewrite that bundle of genetic and psychological information which is us and draw us again on the blackboard of life after we have died.'[27]

Man is a unity of 'soul and body' (Matthew 10:28) and only in this unity is a human being complete. Death brings about a temporary separation of body and soul, but at the Second Coming this separation will end and bodies and souls will be reunited, so that all who have died will be whole human beings again. This tells us that, while people may be said to be 'dead and buried', they are never 'dead and gone'. Instead, 'There will be a resurrection of both the just and the unjust' (Acts 24:15). From then on, everyone concerned will have resurrection bodies, identifiable with those they had on earth, yet not identical to them, but designed to fit their new, eternal destination.

Without explaining how this is to be done (and how could we understand it?), the Bible says that, while both the 'just' and the 'unjust' will be made whole again, what happens to them next will be very different. The souls of unbelievers will be taken from the 'condemned cell' of Hades and reunited with their bodies to face their Maker and receive their final, dreadful sentence. The souls of believers, reunited with their bodies, will also stand before God, not to be condemned, but to be welcomed into an even fuller experience of God's glorious presence than they enjoyed in Paradise.

The Bible also tells us what will happen to those who are still living on earth when Jesus returns. He himself put it like this: 'Two men will be in the field; one will be taken and one left. Two women will be grinding at the mill; one will be taken and one left' (Matthew 24:40-41). On another occasion he spoke of people who would be asleep in bed at the time of his coming and said, 'One will be taken and the other left' (Luke 17:34). Theologians have wrestled for centuries over the precise meaning of this statement, but nobody can doubt that the words 'taken' and 'left' point once again to a great divide. As with those who will have died before Jesus returns, those who are still alive, both believers and unbelievers, will eventually have changed bodies and, as whole persons, will reach one of two final destinations, one of which will be glorious and the other more appalling than words can express.

All we have just seen now brings us to focus our attention on the inescapable fact that God will 'judge the living and the dead' (2 Timothy 4:1). Nothing, not even death, will shield us from standing body and soul before our Maker and Judge. The Bible says, 'It is appointed for man to die once, and after that comes judgement' (Hebrews 9:27), the moment when 'each of us will give an account of himself to God' (Romans 14:12).

The Judge

We now come to an event that is beyond our imagination, yet we are not reduced to guesswork, because the Bible gives a clear outline of what will take place when we face 'the Judge of all the earth' (Genesis 18:25). The basic facts are so certain that the Bible calls the resurrection of the dead and eternal judgement 'elementary doctrine' (Hebrews 6:1). It also tells us that, while 'it is God who executes judgement' (Psalm 75:7), the final judgement of mankind will be carried out by God the Son, the Lord Jesus Christ. Jesus commanded his followers 'to preach to the people and to testify that he is the one appointed by God to be judge of the living and the dead' (Acts 10:42), while elsewhere the Bible declares, 'For we must all appear before the judgement seat of Christ' (2 Corinthians 5:10). The one who will act for the Godhead in pronouncing judgement on us is not some invisible, unfeeling spirit, but someone who knows from personal experience as a human being all the twists and turns, problems and pressures, trials and temptations of life on earth.

Then what are the issues that will determine what happens on the day of final judgement? In the first place there are several facts we need to grasp about God, the Judge.

The first is *his utter perfection*, something on which the Bible insists from cover to cover. We are told that 'The LORD our God is holy!' (Psalm 99:9), that 'The LORD is righteous in all his ways' (Psalm 145:17) and that 'In him is no darkness at all' (1 John 1:5). This perfect holiness is what makes God distinct from every other being. This means that every decision he makes is right, just and perfect and guarantees that 'He will judge the world in righteousness' (Acts 17:31).

Secondly, there is *his omniscience,* his complete and perfect knowledge of everything, including every aspect of our lives here on earth. By 2006 there were over four million CCTV cameras in Britain, roughly one for every fourteen people in the nation. It has been estimated that, outside the privacy of our homes, every person in the land is captured on camera an average of 300 times a day, making Britain one of five countries with 'endemic surveillance'. Yet even so, these cameras see only a small fraction of what we do and nothing of what we say or think. God's complete and perfect knowledge goes far beyond this. The Bible tells us that he is 'perfect in knowledge' (Job 37:16) and that 'No creature is hidden from his sight, but all are naked and exposed to the eyes of him to whom we must give account' (Hebrews 4:13). There will be no 'hidden secrets' on that day, as God 'will bring to light the things now hidden in darkness and will disclose the purposes of the heart' (1 Corinthians 4:5). When the Bible says, 'We must all appear before the judgement seat of Christ' (2 Corinthians 5:10), it is not merely saying that we shall be there. To 'appear' is to be revealed in our true colours, with no possibility of any disguise or deception.

Thirdly, there is *his righteous anger.* God is not a 'soft touch', who can be talked out of his holy opposition to sin of every kind. Any view of God that concentrates only on his love, his mercy or his kindness misses the point that the Bible speaks more of his anger against sin than it does of any of these attributes, and that 'God's wrath is a central piece in the biblical jigsaw.'[28] R. C. Sproul goes so far as to say, 'A God of love who has no wrath is no God. He is an idol of our own making, as much as if we carved him out of stone.'[29] The Bible specifically calls the Day of Judgement 'the day of wrath when God's righteous judgement will be revealed' (Romans 2:5). God's wrath is an expression of his perfect justice.

The judged

Having noted these important truths about the one 'who is to judge the living and the dead' (2 Timothy 4:1), we must now take an honest look at three of the things the Bible tells us about those who are to be judged — that is, about each one of us.

The first is that *we are in a dire moral and spiritual state*. The Bible's most direct way of stating this is to say that 'All have sinned and fall short of the glory of God' (Romans 3:23), and we dare not go any further without coming to a clear understanding of what this means — and what it will mean on the day of final judgement.

It might help to begin with the second part of that statement, which tells us that we 'fall short of the glory of God'. As we saw much earlier in this booklet, man was the summit of creation and, as such, revealed God's glory in a greater way than all the rest of his creation. The apostle Paul takes up this point by defining man as 'the image and glory of God' (1 Corinthians 11:7). The first question in the famous *Westminster Shorter Catechism* is, 'What is the chief end of man?', to which the answer is: 'Man's chief end is to glorify God and to enjoy him for ever.' For some time, our first parents glorified God in their perfect obedience to his will and as a result enjoyed their perfect relationship with him. But Genesis 3 records that at some point they decided to throw off God's authority and go their own way. For the first time they fell short of the glory of God — and all of their natural successors have been doing so ever since. Even at our best we are falling short of the chief purpose for which we were created, which was to reflect God's glory in our lives.

Why is this? What has brought us to this state? Three words supply the answer: '*All have sinned.*' To call anyone a sinner usually brings a firm denial, as we all like to be well thought of. But what is the truth of the matter? Take the Ten Commandments, which even people who never read the Bible think of as being God's standard for human behaviour. How do we measure up to them? Most people think of 'sin' in terms of the sixth and seventh commandments — 'You shall not murder,' and 'You shall not commit adultery' (Exodus 20:13,14). Almost everybody claims to have kept the first of these, while most people would claim to have kept the second. Yet to respond like this is totally to misunderstand what these commandments mean. The Bible says that God's law is not only 'holy and righteous and good', reflecting God's own nature, but also 'spiritual' (Romans 7:12,14). It relates not only to our outward actions, but also to our thoughts, desires and motives.

Jesus made this clear by stating that unjustified anger, contempt and character assassination are murder committed in the heart (see Matthew

5:21-22). He was just as explicit with regard to the command about adultery: 'Everyone who looks at a woman with lustful intent has already committed adultery with her in his heart' (Matthew 5:28). God 'knows the heart' (Acts 15:8) and in his sight even an immoral thought is as sinful as the act of adultery.

A right understanding of these two commandments is challenging enough, but elsewhere he went even further. When someone asked, 'Which commandment is the most important of all?' (Mark 12:28), he replied, 'The most important is, "Hear, O Israel: The Lord our God, the Lord is one. And you shall love the Lord your God with all your heart and with all your soul and with all your mind and with all your strength." The second is this: "You shall love your neighbour as yourself"' (Mark 12:29-31). As we can easily see by looking at the Ten Commandments as they were given in Exodus 20:1-17, this answer perfectly expresses all ten of them, 'the most important' summarizing the first four, which deal with our relationship to God, and 'the second' summarizing the last six, which deal with our relationships with our fellow human beings. Can anybody truthfully claim to have kept these? *Can you?* Have you truly loved God with all your heart, mind, soul and strength? Then, if this is the greatest commandment, aren't you guilty of the greatest sin? The 'second' commandment is equally challenging. Have you always treated other people with the same care and concern that you have taken over your own interests and well-being? If not, haven't you also broken the last six commandments?

The Bible drives this message home in another way: 'For whoever keeps the whole law but fails in one point has become accountable for all of it' (James 2:10). An examination paper may set out ten questions to be answered, but indicate that only six need be attempted. God's law is very different. It is not like a pile of stones, from which one can be removed without anyone noticing its loss. Instead, it is like a pane of glass: one crack, and the whole pane is ruined. We could use other illustrations to make the same point: if one link in a chain snaps, the whole chain is broken; one puncture ruins a whole tyre; one break in a telegraph wire loses all communication. The Bible says, 'If we say we have no sin, we deceive ourselves, and the truth is not in us' (1 John 1:8), and to deny that we have sinned is to add yet another sin to those we have already committed. As far as God's law is concerned, to sin even once is to break all of it.

Secondly, and to emphasize what we have just seen, *our own efforts to get right with God count for nothing*. The Bible puts it like this: 'For all who rely on works of the law are under a curse; for it is written, "Cursed be everyone who does not abide by *all things* written in the Book of the Law, and do them"' (Galatians 3:10, emphasis added). If we rely on our own efforts to get right with God we are certain to fail, because God requires perfect obedience, not partial obedience — and 'Who can say, "I have made my heart pure; I am clean from my sin"?' (Proverbs 20:9). *Can you?*

If the pass mark in an examination is seventy-five per cent, the person who scores seventy per cent is no better off than someone who did not even get fifty per cent: they both fail. A motorist guilty of a speeding offence would not be let off because his car's lights were all in working order, nor would a drug pusher be cleared because he had never robbed a bank. The Bible warns us that 'By works of the law no one will be justified' (Galatians 2:16). God's law reveals sin, but can do nothing to remove it; it condemns us, but is unable to cure us; it exposes us, but never excuses us. The contemporary British preacher John Stott explains why: 'The law cannot save us, for the sole reason that we cannot keep it; and we cannot keep it because of indwelling sin.'[30]

Thirdly, this all means that, left to ourselves, *we are unable to avoid God's anger*; in the Bible's words, 'Those who are in the flesh cannot please God' (Romans 8:8). To be 'in the flesh' is to have self as the controlling force in life. A person who is 'in the flesh' may do many things that are good in themselves, but these are not done because God commands them, or in order to please God. As long as our lives are self-controlled ('This is my life, my time, my money'; 'This is what I think, what I want, what I choose to do'), we are putting self in God's place, and so can never have his approval. We can please other people, such as our employers, family members or friends, but if our lives are controlled by our sinful, self-centred natures we can never please God, either in this life or on the Day of Judgement.

The other place

We have already seen that the Bible divides humankind into 'the righteous' and 'the unrighteous', which in essence means believers and unbelievers. On the Day of Judgement our destiny will depend on which of these applies to us, and the Bible confirms what we have just seen: 'None is righteous, no, not one' (Romans 3:10). The simple truth is that by nature we are rebellious sinners, unfit to stand before a just and holy God. However we try to justify or excuse ourselves, or claim some kind of respectability, we are guilty as charged and in the light of God's law are exposed as self-centred rebels against our Maker. Unless there is an astonishing intervention on our behalf, we are doomed to hear the dreadful words, 'Depart from me, you cursed, into the eternal fire prepared for the devil and his angels,' and to 'go away into eternal punishment' (Matthew 25:41,46). The Bible's major word for this is 'hell'.

Because this biblical picture is so appalling some people take great care not to use the word 'hell' in a casual or careless way and are disturbed when this is done, yet others have no such scruples. People speak of 'a hell of a good meal', 'a hell of a long flight', or 'a hell of a bad accident'. The word is now spread so thinly over the English language that its original meaning is largely ignored, while many who cheerfully speak about heaven try to dilute the alternative by referring to hell as 'the other place'.

Over the centuries, artists, authors and others have painted terrifying images of what hell is like, but we should ignore all human speculation and concentrate only on what the Bible says. Most of the direct teaching about hell as the final destiny of the unrighteous is found in the New Testament. It may surprise many people to know that Jesus spoke more about judgement and hell than about any other topic and that more than half of the forty parables he told relate to the final judgement. Some people try to shy away from the subject by claiming that their idea of Christianity is the Sermon on the Mount, yet it was in that sermon that Jesus warned people of 'the hell of fire' (Matthew 5:22), of the danger of being 'thrown into hell' (Matthew 5:29) and of the need to turn from the kind of life 'that leads to destruction' (Matthew 7:13). It is impossible to read what Jesus taught in that one sermon alone without facing the fact that hell is not a figment of religious imagination but a terrifying reality. From all the images the New Testament uses to give us a picture of hell, it will be sufficient to look very briefly at six.

Firstly, it is like *a rubbish dump*. In New Testament times the Valley of Hinnom, just south-east of Jerusalem and now called Wadi-al-Rababi, was a public rubbish dump, into which all the city's offal and filth was poured. Later, the bodies of animals and the corpses of criminals were flung there and left to rot or to be consumed by the fire that was always burning. The Jewish name for this noxious place was *Ge Hinnom*, and this is the root of *Gehenna*, the word Jesus used eleven times to speak about the eternal destiny of the unrighteous. However much we wince at the thought, hell is like a cosmic rubbish dump, and all who go there become the garbage of the universe, wasted and worthless. C. S. Lewis goes so far as to say, 'To enter hell is to be banished from humanity. What is cast (or casts itself) into hell is not man; it is "remains".'[31]

Secondly, it is like *a prison*. In a parable about a king's servant who was sent to prison for cruel and unforgiving behaviour, Jesus warned his hearers that unless they changed their ways God would do the same 'to every one of you' (Matthew 18:35). Elsewhere, the apostle Peter says that God knows how to 'keep the unrighteous under punishment until the day of judgement' (2 Peter 2:9) and, as this 'remand cell' is described as having 'chains of gloomy darkness' (2 Peter 2:4), we can be sure that the final state of these prisoners will be no better.

Thirdly, it is *a place of darkness*. One Old Testament writer describes it as 'the land of darkness and deep shadow, the land of gloom like thick darkness, like deep shadow without any order, where light is as thick darkness' (Job 10:21-22), while Jesus spoke of the unrighteous being 'thrown into the outer darkness' (Matthew 8:12). As he spoke not merely of 'darkness' but of *'the* outer darkness', he clearly meant something infinitely worse than any physical, moral or spiritual darkness ever experienced here on earth.

Fourthly, Jesus said that the unrighteous would spend eternity in *a place where 'their worm does not die'* (Mark 9:48). To speak of 'their' worm' points to an internal, never-ending punishment. Those whose destiny is hell will have a capacity for suffering far beyond anything they had on earth, not least because their guilty and polluted consciences will be their worst tormentors. They will have constant and total recall of their every thought, word and deed while on earth and will be agonizingly aware that they deliberately chose the lifestyle that has now condemned them. As C. S. Lewis powerfully puts it, 'The doors of hell are locked on the inside.'[32]

Fifthly, Jesus said that in hell *there will be weeping and gnashing of teeth* (Matthew 8:12). In the original language, the word translated 'there' is emphatic, meaning 'in that place'. Jesus was saying that any 'weeping and gnashing of teeth' we experience on earth is as nothing compared with what happens in hell. I remember standing at the Vietnam War Memorial in Washington, DC, a black granite wall inscribed with the names of 57,939 American service personnel who died in that disastrous conflict. As I stood there a man kneeled in front of one of those names, tears rolling down his cheeks. How many tears have now been shed over the horrendous loss of life caused by wars? How many have been shed at hospital beds, at accident sites and over marriage breakdowns, to say nothing of those caused by rumour, malicious gossip, grinding poverty, tension and depression? There is simply no way of quantifying this, yet all of these tears are as nothing compared to the tears that will be shed 'there'. The seventeenth-century English preacher Ralph Venning was not exaggerating when he wrote, 'The gripings and grindings of all the diseases and torments that men can or do suffer in this life are like flea bites to it.'[33]

Sixthly, hell is likened to *fire*, a picture the Bible uses over twenty times. Old Testament writers warned of 'fire and sulphur' (Psalm 11:6), 'a stream of sulphur' (Isaiah 30:33), 'consuming fire' and 'everlasting burnings' (Isaiah 33:14), and of God's wrath being 'poured out like fire' (Nahum 1:6). Nor can we dismiss this as 'Old Testament teaching, and not the kind of thing Jesus taught', because in the New Testament nobody uses the image of fire more frequently than he did. He warned certain people that they were 'liable to the hell of fire' (Matthew 5:22), while elsewhere he spoke of those who would be thrown 'into the fiery furnace' (Matthew 13:42) and 'into the eternal fire' (Matthew 18:8).

The imagery is frightening, yet it is only a picture of something even more terrifying — *the presence of God!* People tend to think of the unrighteous being 'eternally separated from God', but this phrase never occurs in the Bible. Instead, it tells us that the worst horror of the unrighteous will be to be eternally faced with the glory, majesty, authority and power of the one they rejected while on earth, and who is 'a consuming fire' (Hebrews 12:29). They will be 'tormented with fire and sulphur in the presence of the holy angels *and in the presence of the Lamb*' (Revelation 14:10, emphasis added) and, as 'the Lamb' is a common title for the Lord Jesus Christ, the Judge of all mankind, this confirms that his presence will be a fearful reality for them. As the seventeenth-century English preacher John Flavel put it, 'The worst terrors of the prisoners in hell come from the presence of the Lamb.'[34] The twentieth-century French philosopher Jean-Paul Sartre, who was brought up in church circles but later 'stopped associating' with God and became an icon of atheism, grasped something of this: 'The last thing I want is to be subject to the unremitting gaze of a holy God.'[35]

Yet this will be the appalling fate of all who are in hell. They will be exposed to the awesome fire of God's righteous and unrestricted anger, unleashed against them in the way their sinfulness deserves and his holiness demands. They will never again have so much as a glimmer of these things, all of which they rejected while on earth.

One other thing will make hell even worse: *those who are sent there will remain there for ever.* Over the centuries, there have been many attempts to find a way out for its prisoners. These have included annihilation (bringing all suffering to an end) or reincarnation (bringing people back to earth to improve their *karma*), but we have already seen that these ideas can be dismissed. Some have suggested that hell is a kind of 'finishing school', in which the suffering of the unrighteous purges them and prepares them for heaven, but this notion has no biblical basis. Nor has the idea of purgatory, a fifteenth-century invention by the Roman Catholic Church. This rather complex doctrine lists five potential places to which human souls go immediately after death, in one of which they are punished and purified until fit to be transferred to heaven. The Bible knows nothing of this. It speaks of 'eternal fire' (Matthew 25:41) and 'eternal punishment' (Matthew 25:46) and of the unrighteous being 'tormented day and night *for ever and ever*' (Revelation 20:10, emphasis added). The twentieth-century American theologian

Loraine Boettner could not have put it better: 'If these expressions do not teach that the punishment of the wicked continues eternally, it is difficult to see how it could be taught in human language.'[36] In hell, there is no such thing as an hour, a day, a week, a month or a year. It is literally never-ending.

Escape route

For anyone who has grasped what has been said in this booklet so far, one question should dominate all others: 'How can I escape such a terrible fate?' The Bible asks precisely that question — and the answer lies within the question: 'How shall we escape if we neglect such a great salvation?' (Hebrews 2:3). We have already seen our need to be saved from the horrors of hell, but what exactly is this 'great salvation'?

It would obviously need to be a means of forgiving all our sin and *paying its penalty in full on our behalf.* Yet only God can truly grant forgiveness, as he is the one who has been wronged by every sin we have ever committed. When Joseph, later to become a high-ranking official in Egypt, was tempted by his boss's wife to commit adultery with her, he protested: 'How ... can I do this great wickedness *and sin against God*? (Genesis 39:9, emphasis added). When King David of Israel confessed that he had committed adultery and murder he cried out to God, 'Against you, *you only*, have I sinned' (Psalm 51:4, emphasis added). In the New Testament we read that when two religious hypocrites, Ananias and Sapphira, tried to deceive the apostles about the amount of their contribution to church funds, they were told, 'You have not lied to men but to God' (Acts 5:4). Every sin, from a 'white lie' to murder, is an offence committed against God. This means that God alone can fully forgive sin and provide a substitute capable of paying the penalty for the sins of all men.

Yet the substitute would also have to be *a sinless human being* — sinless so that the penalty paid would not be for the substitute's own sin but for the sins of others, and human because only in a human body and soul could the double death penalty of physical and spiritual death be paid.

The greatest news ever revealed to the human race is this — *there is such a substitute!* This is the Bible's central message from cover to cover, but there are places where the whole stupendous story is put into a few words: 'While we were still weak, at the right time Christ died for the ungodly' (Romans 5:6); 'God shows his love for us in that while we were still sinners, Christ died for us' (Romans 5:8); 'This is how God showed his love among us: He sent his one and only Son into the world that we might live through him' (1 John 4:9, NIV).

Two truths hold all of this together. The first is that *Jesus Christ is God*. The Bible's message is not that God sent a third party to rescue us from the power and penalty of sin, but that he himself came. Jesus clearly claimed to be God — 'I and the Father are one' (John 10:30); 'Whoever sees me sees him who sent me' (John 12:45) — and his whole life endorsed his claims. He was completely 'without sin' (Hebrews 4:15). Even as a twelve-year old he spoke with such authority that experienced theologians were 'amazed at his understanding and his answers' (Luke 2:47). Whenever he chose to do so, he was able to heal 'every disease and every affliction among the people' (Matthew 4:24) and on several occasions he actually raised the dead. What is more, he assured certain people, 'Your sins are forgiven' (Matthew 9:2) and said of those who trusted him, 'I give them eternal life' (John 10:28). As only God can remove the guilt of sin and declare that it has been removed, and only God can grant eternal life, these two actions point powerfully to the truth that Jesus Christ is God. The Bible confirms this again and again, declaring that 'He is the image of the invisible God' (Colossians 1:15). To deny that Jesus is divine is to reject the authority of the Bible.

The second truth is that *Jesus Christ became a man*, adding humanity to his deity and from then onwards remaining both God and man. Though without a human father, he was 'born of woman' (Galatians 4:4) and grew from childhood to manhood like any other male. He had to be taught to walk, speak, write and dress. We are specifically told that he was hungry, thirsty, tired and weakened by suffering. He expressed love and anger, joy and sorrow. He prayed and fasted, studied the Old Testament Scriptures (he frequently quoted them from memory) and attended public worship. He was also 'tempted in every way, just as we are' (Hebrews 4:15, NIV) — and, as 'God cannot be tempted with evil' (James 1:13), we can be sure that Jesus was not 'God in a skin', but as fully human as any other person living on our planet.

It is this Jesus, fully God and fully man, who is our only means of escape from the horrors of hell: 'Christ Jesus came into the world to save sinners' (1 Timothy 1:15); and 'There is no other name under heaven given among men by which we must be saved' (Acts 4:12). But what did he do that saves people from going to hell and ensures that they will go to heaven? The Bible's answer is that in his life and death he fulfilled all the demands of God's law on behalf of others.

Firstly, *he lived the perfect life God's law demands.* He never thought, said or did anything that was not completely in tune with God's perfect will. He was able to say, 'I always do the things that are pleasing to him' (John 8:29), while someone who had spent three years in his close company testified, 'He committed no sin, neither was deceit found in his mouth' (1 Peter 2:22). Another New Testament writer underlines this by saying that Jesus was 'holy, innocent, unstained, separated from sinners' (Hebrews 7:26). Every virtue known to man was present in his life, and every vice known to man was absent from his life — and he lived that perfect life in order to meet all the demands of God's holy law on behalf of others.

Secondly, *he paid in full the death penalty God's law demands.* Time and again the Bible underlines its message that 'The wages of sin is death' (Romans 6:23), yet in his death Jesus paid those 'wages' in full, even though there was not a trace of sin in his life. On the face of it, his death seems both illogical and immoral, but it was neither, because Jesus voluntarily died not for his own sin, but for the sins of others: 'Christ ... suffered once for sins, the righteous for the unrighteous, that he might bring us to God' (1 Peter 3:18). This is the very essence of the Christian gospel: *Jesus died in the place of sinners and on their behalf.* He became as accountable for their sins as if he had been responsible for them, and he paid in full the penalty that was due.

Not only did he die physically by being crucified, but as he was dying he cried, 'My God, my God, why have you forsaken me?' (Matthew 27:46). What Jesus endured in that agonizing moment is utterly beyond our understanding, but we do know that he experienced the full impact of God's terrible wrath against the sinners he represented and the sins they had committed. This is the 'great salvation' that God offers to guilty, lost and helpless sinners. What is more, it is the *only* way of salvation: 'And there is salvation in no one else, for there is no other name under heaven given among men by which we must be saved' (Acts 4:12).

If this was the end of the Bible's message it might leave us moved by such an amazing sacrifice, but still baffled as to how we might benefit from it. But it is not the end of the story! After three days (and exactly as he had prophesied) Jesus rose again from the dead and over a period of seven weeks (before he went back to heaven) met with hundreds of friends and followers, providing 'many convincing proofs that he was alive' (Acts 1:3, NIV). The evidence for the resurrection is so overwhelming that Lord Darling, a former Chief Justice of England, once wrote, 'There exists such overwhelming evidence, positive and negative, factual and circumstantial, that no intelligent jury in the world could fail to bring in a verdict that the resurrection story is true.'[37]

Not only was Jesus 'declared to be the Son of God … by his resurrection from the dead' (Romans 1:4), but his resurrection is proof that all the demands of God's holy law had been met, his justice completely satisfied and his holy anger against those for whom Jesus died vented in full.

Escape!

At one stage in Old Testament history, God's message through Moses was this: 'I call heaven and earth to witness against you today, that I have set before you life and death, blessing and curse. Therefore choose life' (Deuteronomy 30:19). As you reach the end of this booklet, I urge you to face that choice — and to make the right one!

Your final destiny is at stake, with heaven and hell as the only alternatives. Left to your own efforts, even the most religious or respectable of them, you are doomed to hear the dreadful words, 'Depart from me … into the eternal fire' (Matthew 25:41), and to be exposed to God's awesome anger for ever — but there is an alternative! In his amazing grace, God has made a way for sinful rebels to return to him and to enjoy eternity in his glorious presence. Jesus came, lived, died and rose again 'to bring us to God', to deliver sinners immediately from the penalty of sin, gradually from its power and eventually from its very presence — in heaven, where 'Death shall be no more, neither shall there be mourning nor crying nor pain' (Revelation 21:4). It is literally impossible to describe the glories or the delights of heaven, where the righteous will enjoy permanently the fulness of God's love. Never doubt God's overwhelming love for sinners, 'not wishing that any should perish' (2 Peter 3:9), but, equally, never doubt his perfect justice in condemning those who reject his love.

Only one question remains: how can you escape the horrors of hell and enjoy the glories of heaven? Everything the Bible says on the subject can be summed up in these words: 'For God so loved the world, that he gave his only Son, that whoever believes in him should not perish but have eternal life' (John 3:16). The key word here is 'believes'. To 'believe' in Jesus Christ is not merely to agree that certain things about him are true, nor even to accept that he is the Son of God. In the first place it involves admitting to him that you are a sinner in need of a Saviour, having a heartfelt sorrow for your sins, and having a genuine desire to turn from sin and to live a life that is honouring to God and obedient to his Word. The Bible calls this 'repentance' and Jesus himself said, 'Unless you repent, you will ... perish' (Luke 13:5).

Then it means trusting in Jesus Christ, and in him alone, to save you from the guilt and consequences of your sins. It means committing yourself to him, relying only and utterly on him to save you from the fate that will otherwise be yours. There is no escape from the wrath of God except in the one who bore that wrath on behalf of those who put their trust in him. The person who refuses to do so 'is condemned already, because he has not believed in the name of the only Son of God' (John 3:18). In the light of that terrible warning I urge you to respond personally to his amazing love and grace.

The Bible promises that 'Everyone who calls on the name of the Lord will be saved' (Romans 10:13). Then call upon him now! Ask him to enable you to turn from sin and to put your trust in him alone for your salvation, claiming his promise that everyone who truly does so 'has eternal life and will not be condemned; he has crossed over from death to life' (John 5:24, NIV).

Where do *you* go from here?

1. Svetlana Alliluyeva, *Twenty Letters to a Friend*, Hutchinson.

2. *Golf World*, January 2008.

3. J. I. Packer, *Knowing God*, Hodder & Stoughton, p.172.

4. Bernard of Clairvaux, cited by Thomas Brooks, *The Complete Works*, The Banner of Truth Trust, vol. 1, p.225.

5. Cited by Dave Hunt, *Whatever Happened to Heaven?*, Harvest House Publishers, p.14.

6. Robert Morley, *Around the World in 81 Years*, Coronet Press, p.176.

7. Aristotle, *Nicomachean Ethics*, 3:9.

8. Epicurus, 'Letter to Menoeceus', in *Letters, Principal Doctrines and Vatican Sayings*, trans. Russel M. Geer.

9. Cited by J. W. N. Sullivan, *The Limitations of Science*, Pelican, p.175.

10. Tony Benn, *More Time for Politics*, Hutchinson, p.25.

11. Cited by Michael Green, *Man Alive!*, Inter-Varsity Press, p.12.

12 . As above.

13. John Lennon, *Imagine*, Amsco Wyse.

14. Francis A. Schaeffer, *Death in the City*, Inter-Varsity Press, pp.86-7.

15. David Watson, *Is Anyone There?*, Hodder & Stoughton, p.66.

16. Douglas Kelly, *Creation and Change*, Christian Focus Publications, p.219.

17. Peter Lewis, *The Message of the Living God*, Inter-Varsity Press, p.59.

18 . Sheldon Vanauken, *A Severe Mercy*, Hodder & Stoughton, p.203.

19. See Peter Alliss, *An Autobiography*, Collins, p.128.

20. R. C. Sproul, *Reason to Believe*, Lamplighter Books, Zondervan, pp.99-100.

21. Cited by Professor William Hendricks, in 'Death: A Theological Perspective', a lecture given at South Western Baptist Theological Seminary, Fort Worth, Texas, 26 October 1976.

22. Lewis, *The Message of the Living God*, p.78.

23. *The Independent*, 31 May 1990.

24. Francis A. Schaeffer, *Genesis in Time and Space*, Hodder & Stoughton, p.101 (emphasis added).

25. Bruce Milne, *Know the Truth*, Inter-Varsity Press, p.255.

26. C. S. Lewis, *Mere Christianity*, McMillan, p.50.

27. John Benton, *How Can a God of Love Send People to Hell?*, Evangelical Press, p.125 (emphasis added).

28. William Eisenhower, 'Sleepers in the Hands of an Angry God', *Christianity Today*, 20 March 1987.

29. R. C. Sproul, *The Holiness of God*, Tyndale House Publishers, p.228.

30. John R. W. Stott, *Men made New*, Inter-Varsity Fellowship, p.70

31. C. S. Lewis, *The Problem of Pain*, Macmillan, p.125.

32. As above, p.127.

33. Ralph Venning, *The Plague of Plagues*, The Banner of Truth Trust, p.79.

34. John Flavel, Works, The Banner of Truth Trust, vol. 3, p.142.

35. Cited by Larry Dixon, *The Other Side of the Good News*, Victor Books, p.162.

36. Loraine Boettner, *Immortality*, The Presbyterian & Reformed Publishing Company, p.120.
37. Cited by Green, *Man Alive!*, p.54.